D1625608

When I Loved myself enough

KIM McMILLEN
with Alison McMillen

To my Ali girl

An extraordinary daughter
who always knew I wasn't
born yesterday

INTRODUCTION

For many years I lived with a guarded heart. I did not know how to extend love and compassion to myself. In my fortieth year that began changing.

As I grew to love all of who I am, life started changing in beautiful and mysterious ways. My heart softened and I began to see through very different eyes.

My commitment to follow this calling grew strong and in the process a divine intelligence came to guide my life. I believe this ever-present resource is grace, and is available to us all.

For the past twelve years I have been learning to recognize and accept this gift. Cultivating love and compassion for myself made it possible.

The following steps are uniquely mine. Yours will look different. But I do hope mine give voice to a hunger you may share.

When I loved myself enough

I quit settling for too little.

When I loved myself enough

I came to know my own goodness.

When I loved myself enough

I began taking the gift of life
seriously and gratefully.

When I loved myself enough

I began to know I was in the
right place at the right time
and I could relax.

When I loved myself enough

I felt compelled to slow down —
way down.

And that has made all the
difference.

When I loved myself enough

I bought a feather bed.

When I loved myself enough

I came to love being alone
surrounded by silence,
awed by its spell,
listening to inner space.

When I loved myself enough

I came to see I am not special
but I am unique.

When I loved myself enough

I redefined success and life
became simple. Oh, the
pleasure of that.

When I loved myself enough

I came to know I am worthy
of knowing God directly.

When I loved myself enough

I began to see I didn't have
to chase after life. If I am
quiet and hold still, life
comes to me.

When I loved myself enough

I gave up the belief that
life is hard.

When I loved myself enough

I came to see emotional pain
is a signal I am operating
outside truth.

When I loved myself enough

I let the tomboy in me swing
off the rope in Jackass Canyon.
Yes!

When I loved myself enough

I learned to meet my own
needs and not call it selfish.

When I loved myself enough

The parts of me long-ignored,
the orphans of my soul, quit
vying for attention. That was
the beginning of inner peace.
Then I began seeing clearly.

When I loved myself enough

I began to see that desires
of the heart do come, and
I grew more patient and calm,
except when I forgot.

When I loved myself enough

I quit ignoring or tolerating
my pain.

When I loved myself enough

I started feeling all my feelings,
not analysing them — really
feeling them.

When I do, something amazing
happens. Try it. You will see.

When I loved myself enough

My heart became so tender
it could welcome joy and
sorrow equally.

When I loved myself enough

I started meditating every day.
This is a profound act of self-love.

When I loved myself enough

I came to feel like a gift to the world and I collected beautiful ribbons and bows.

They still hang on my wall to remind me.

When I loved myself enough

I learned to ask 'Who in me
is feeling this way?' when I feel
anxious, angry, restless or sad.

If I listen patiently I discover
who needs my love.

When I loved myself enough

I no longer needed things or
people to make me feel safe.

When I loved myself enough

I quit wishing my life looked
some other way and began to
see that as it is, my life serves
my evolution.

When I loved myself enough

I began to comprehend the
complexity, mystery and vastness
of my soul. How foolish to think
I can know the meaning of
another's life.

When I loved myself enough

I quit projecting my strengths and weaknesses on to others and kept them as my own.

When I loved myself enough

I began to feel a divine presence
in me and hear its guidance.

I am learning to trust this and
live from it.

When I loved myself enough

I quit exhausting myself by
trying so hard.

When I loved myself enough

I began to feel a community within. This inner team with diverse talents and idiosyncracies is my strength and my potential.

We hold team meetings.

When I loved myself enough

I stopped blaming myself for choices I had made — which made me feel safe and I took responsibility for them.

When I loved myself enough

I began seeing the abuse in trying to force something or someone who isn't ready — including me.

When I loved myself enough

I began walking and taking the stairs every chance I got, and choosing the scenic route.

When I loved myself enough

I became my own authority by listening to the wisdom of my heart. This is how God speaks to me. This is intuition.

When I loved myself enough

I began feeling such relief.

When I loved myself enough

The impulsive part of me learned
to wait for the right time. Then
I become clear and unafraid.

When I loved myself enough

I began to accept the unacceptable.

When I loved myself enough

I began to see that my ego is part
of my soul. With this shift in
perception it lost its stridency
and paranoia, and could do its job.

When I loved myself enough

I would sometimes wake in the
night to music playing within me.

When I loved myself enough

I began leaving whatever wasn't healthy. This meant people, jobs, my own beliefs and habits — anything that kept me small. My judgement called it disloyal. Now I see it as self-loving.

When I loved myself enough

I gave up perfectionism — that
killer of joy.

When I loved myself enough

I could tell the truth about
my gifts and my limitations.

When I loved myself enough

I quit answering the telephone
when I don't want to talk.

When I loved myself enough

Forgiving others became
irrelevant.

When I loved myself enough

I could remember, during times
of confusion, struggle or grief,
that these too are part of me
and deserve my love.

When I loved myself enough

I could allow my heart to burst
wide open and take in the
pain of the world.

When I loved myself enough

I started picking up litter
on the street.

When I loved myself enough

I could feel God in me and
see God in you. That makes
us divine!

Are you ready for that?

When I loved myself enough

I started writing about my life
and views because I knew this
was my right and my responsibility.

When I loved myself enough

I began to see my purpose
and gently wean myself from
distractions.

When I loved myself enough

I saw that what I resisted
persisted like a small child
tugging my skirt. Now I am
curious and gentle when
resistance comes tugging.

When I loved myself enough

I learned to stop what I am
doing, if even for a moment,
and comfort the part of me
that is sacred.

When I loved myself enough

I learned to say no when I want
to and yes when I want to.

When I loved myself enough

I saw beyond right and wrong
and became neutral. At first
I thought this was indifference;
now I see the clarity that
comes with neutrality.

When I loved myself enough

I began to feed my hunger for
solitude and revel in the
inexplicable contentment that
is its companion.

When I loved myself enough

I could see how funny life is,
how funny I am and how
funny you are.

When I loved myself enough

I recognized my courage and fear,
my naivety and wisdom, and
I make a place for each at
my table.

When I loved myself enough

I started treating myself to a
massage at least once a month.

When I loved myself enough

I realized I am never alone.

When I loved myself enough

I stopped fearing empty time
and quit making plans. Now I do
what feels right and am in step
with my own rhythms.

Delicious!

When I loved myself enough

I quit trying to impress
my brother.

When I loved myself enough

I stopped trying to banish the
critical voices from my head.
Now I say, 'Thank you for your
views' and they feel heard.
End of discussion.

When I loved myself enough

I let the part of me that still misses Kent feel sad instead of trying to stop her from loving him.

When I loved myself enough

I began buying a hostess fruit pie
for the teenager in me who loves
them so. Once in a while, cherry.

When I loved myself enough

I quit trying to be a saviour
for others.

When I loved myself enough

I lost my fear of speaking my truth for I have come to see how good it is.

When I loved myself enough

I began pouring my feelings into
my journals. These loving
companions speak my language.
No translation needed.

When I loved myself enough

I stopped seeking 'experts' and
started living my life.

When I loved myself enough

I came to see how my anger
teaches about responsibility
and my arrogance teaches
about humility, so I listen
to both carefully.

When I loved myself enough

I started eating organically
grown food (except for those
occasional fruit pies of course).

When I loved myself enough

I could be at ease with the
comings and goings of
judgement and despair.

When I loved myself enough

I was able to be treated to a
$50 haircut and enjoy every
minute of it.

When I loved myself enough

I quit having to be right
which makes being wrong
meaningless.

When I loved myself enough

I learned to grieve for the hurts
in life when they happen instead
of making my heart heavy from
lugging them around.

When I loved myself enough

I forgave myself for all the times
I thought I wasn't good enough.

When I loved myself enough

Things got real quiet inside.
Nice. Real nice.

When I loved myself enough

I began listening to the wisdom
of my body. It speaks so clearly
through its fatigue, sensitivities,
aversions and hungers.

When I loved myself enough

I quit fearing my fear.

When I loved myself enough

I quit rehashing the past and
worrying about the future which
keeps me in the present where
aliveness lives.

When I loved myself enough

I realized my mind can ~~torment~~
and deceive me, but in the
service of my heart it is a great
and noble ally.

When I loved myself enough

I began to taste freedom.

When I loved myself enough

I found my voice and wrote
this little book.

About the Author

My mother died in September of 1996, at the age of 52, only a few short months after writing this book. She was not ill and did not know that she was going to die. Her death was very sudden and it deeply shocked everyone who knew her. It has been very difficult for me, as well as her friends and family, to cope with life without her. She died too young, and I am aware of her absence every waking moment.

One thing that has made grieving for her more tolerable has been this book. Following her lead, I continued to publish it out of my home. It has been extremely rewarding work. I have recieved countless letters and phone calls from people all over the world who have been touched by the wisdom of my mom's words. They tell me that they feel as though, through the book, they have come to know Kim McMillen. I could not agree more.

This book is my mother. Its message is what she spent years meditating on, reading and writing about, and experiencing. It is everything she believed in, and everything she brought me up to believe in. It is her autobiography, her declaration, her <u>soul</u>.

Even though she didn't know she was nearing the end of her life, she knew on some level that she had to express the things that she had learned to be true. After many years filled with self-doubt and self-criticism, she decided to devote herself to finding self-compassion. When she did, and was able to write her findings down for others to read, her life was complete, and sadly came to an end.

I have a constant ache in my heart, a longing to see her again in this world. She was an amazing mother, friend, writer, business consultant, chaplain, river runner, dog lover, neighbor and woman. Although I miss her terribly, I am comforted by the knowledge that, as this book is the truest expression of who my mom was; in its continued existence, what she had to offer to the world will live on.

Alison Mcmillen, January 2001

Acknowledgements

I wish to express my deepest thanks to all the people who helped to keep the book alive for the past four years:

My dad, Todd McMillen, Jeffy Griffin & John Davis, Myrta Velez, John Boyer, Jill Jones, Penny Triggs, Win & Cynda Johnson and many others who have helped the book's creation and distribution, not to mention my sanity.

In addition, many many thanks to Jennifer Enderlin, who had the vision to take the book into the big leagues.

Thank you all, this could not have happened without you!

Alin

First published in the USA 1996 by Kim McMillen

First published in Great Britain 2001 by Sidgwick & Jackson
an imprint of Pan Macmillan
20 New Wharf Road, London N1 9RR
Associated companies throughout the world
www.panmacmillan.com

Published in association with St Martin's Press

ISBN 978-0-283-07337-3

Copyright © Kim McMillen 1996
Additional material copyright © Alison McMillen 2001

The right of Kim McMillen to be identified as the
author of this work has been asserted by her in accordance
with the Copyright, Designs and Patents Act 1988.

Calligraphy by Stephen Raw
Illustrations by Andrew Kulman

20

A CIP catalogue record for this book is available from
the British Library.

Printed in Italy

Acknowledgements

I wish to express my deepest thanks to all
the people who helped to keep the book alive
for the past four years:

My dad, Todd McMillen, Jeffy Griffin & John
Davis, Myrta Velez, John Boyer, Jill Jones,
Penny Triggs, Win & Cynda Johnson and many
others who have helped the book's creation and
distribution, not to mention my sanity.

In addition, many many thanks to
Jennifer Enderlin, who had the vision to
take the book into the big leagues.

Thankyou all, this could not have
happened without you!

Alin

First published in the USA 1996 by Kim McMillen

First published in Great Britain 2001 by Sidgwick & Jackson
an imprint of Pan Macmillan
20 New Wharf Road, London N1 9RR
Associated companies throughout the world
www.panmacmillan.com

Published in association with St Martin's Press

ISBN 978-0-283-07337-3

Copyright © Kim McMillen 1996
Additional material copyright © Alison McMillen 2001

The right of Kim McMillen to be identified as the
author of this work has been asserted by her in accordance
with the Copyright, Designs and Patents Act 1988.

Calligraphy by Stephen Raw
Illustrations by Andrew Kulman

20

A CIP catalogue record for this book is available from
the British Library.

Printed in Italy